Common Word Family __it

Vocabulary:

bit

fit

hit

kit

lit

pit

sit

slit

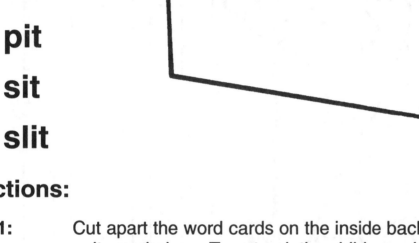

Directions:

Page 1: Cut apart the word cards on the inside back cover and review the __it vocabulary. To extend, the child can draw pictures on corresponding cards and play a matching memory game.

Pages 2-4: Child writes the vocabulary words on the tool kits three times each and colors them. If you have access to a duplicating machine, the tool kits can be copied, cut out, and stapled together to make a book.

Page 5: Child circles the vocabulary words in the word search. They can be found across or down. Child can then color the picture.

Page 6: Child writes the words in alphabetical order onto the tools in the tool kit. Child can then color the picture.

Page 7: Child writes each word two times on the lines provided. Child then fills in the sentence blanks with the words and reads the rebus sentences.

Write each word three times.   Color the tool kit.

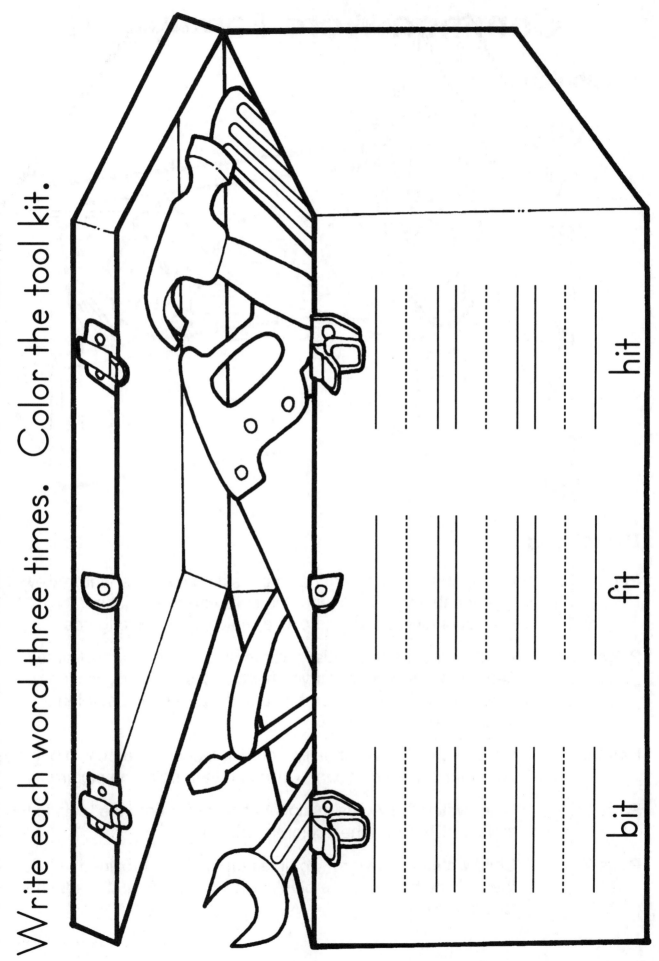

hit

fit

bit

Write each word three times. Color the tool kit.

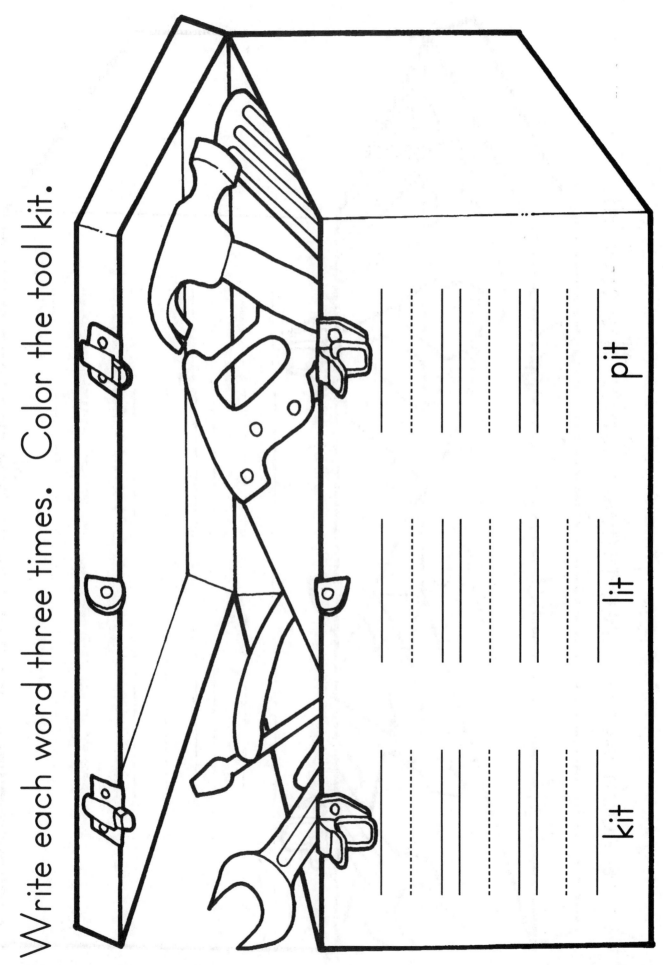

pit

lit

kit

Write each word three times. Color the tool kit.

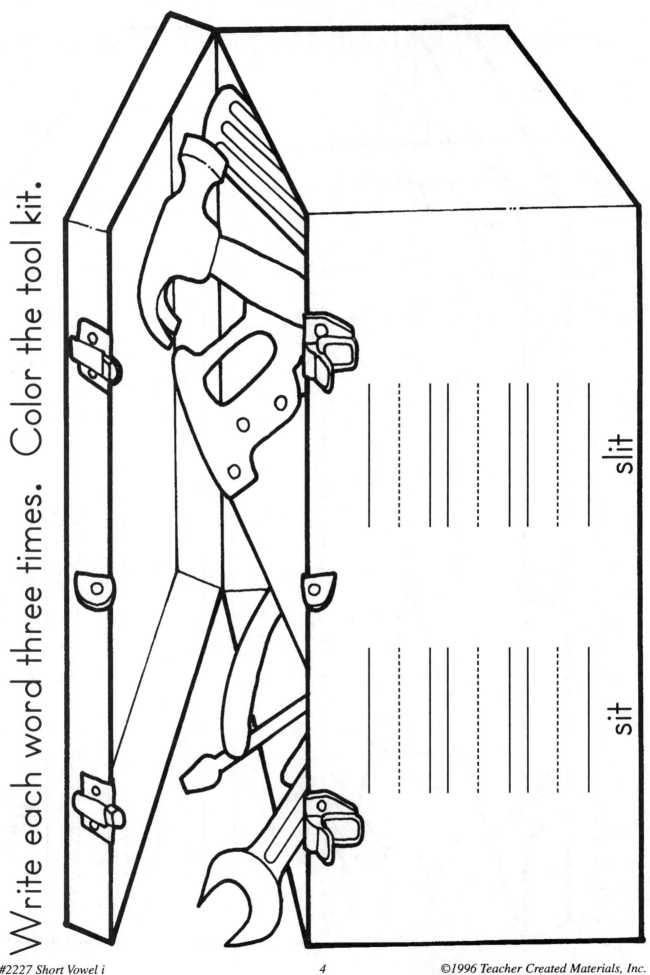

slit

sit

4

Circle each word in the puzzle. Color the picture.

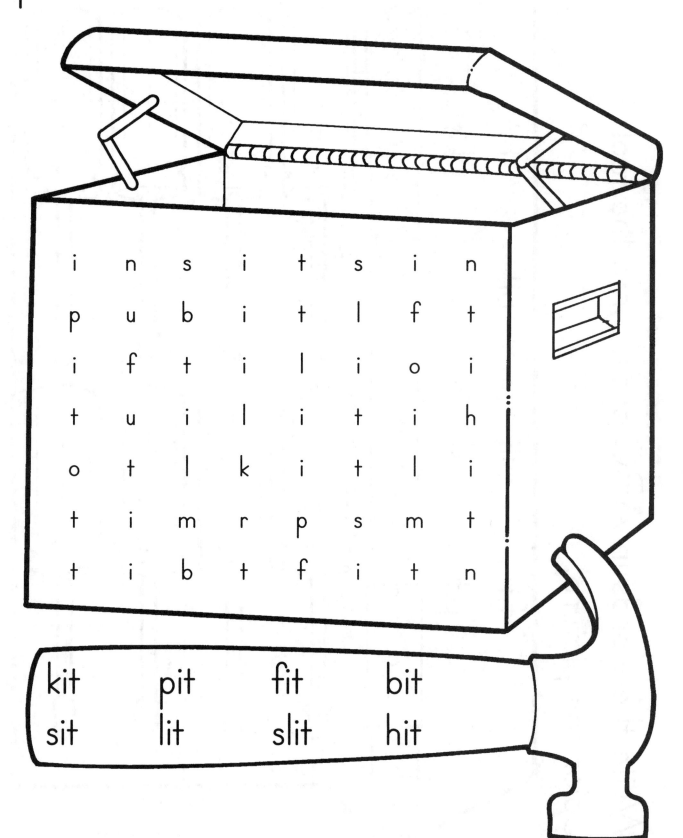

i	n	s	i	t	s	i	n
p	u	b	i	t	l	f	t
i	f	t	i	l	i	o	i
t	u	i	l	i	t	i	h
o	t	l	k	i	t	l	i
t	i	m	r	p	s	m	t
t	i	b	t	f	i	t	n

kit   pit   fit   bit

sit   lit   slit   hit

Write the words in ABC order onto the tools in the kit. Color the picture.

fit   lit   bit   hit

pit   slit   sit   kit

a b c d e f g h i j k l m n o p q r s t u v w x y z

1.

2.

3.

4.

5.

6.

7.

8.

Write each word two times. Then write the word in the sentence.

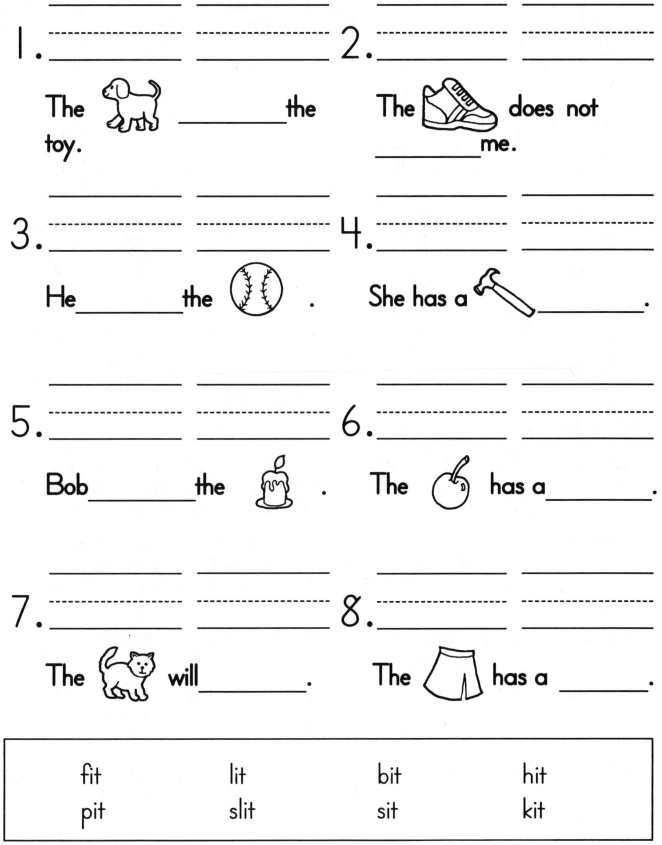

1. _____ _____

The 🐕 _____ the toy.

2. _____ _____

The 👟 does not _____ me.

3. _____ _____

He _____ the ⚾ .

4. _____ _____

She has a 🔨 _____.

5. _____ _____

Bob _____ the 🕯 .

6. _____ _____

The 🍒 has a _____.

7. _____ _____

The 🐱 will _____.

8. _____ _____

The 👖 has a _____.

fit	lit	bit	hit
pit	slit	sit	kit

Common Word Family __in

Vocabulary:

bin

din

fin

pin

tin

win

chin

thin

Directions:

Page 8: Cut apart the word cards on the inside back cover and review the __in vocabulary. To extend, the child can draw pictures on corresponding cards and play a matching memory game.

Pages 9-11: Child writes the vocabulary words on the fish three times each and colors them. If you have access to a duplicating machine, the fish can be copied, cut out, and stapled together to make a book.

Page 12: Child writes the words in the bubbles in alphabetical order. Child can then color the picture.

Page 13: Child colors and cuts out the fish and the circle. Cut out the fish's eye. Attach the circle behind the fish at the dots with a brad. Turn the circle to read and review the __in vocabulary.

Page 15: Child circles the vocabulary words in the word search. They can be found across or down. Child can then color the picture.

Write each word three times. Color the fish.

bin

din

fin

Write each word three times. Color the fish.

pin

tin

win

Write each word three times. Color the fish.

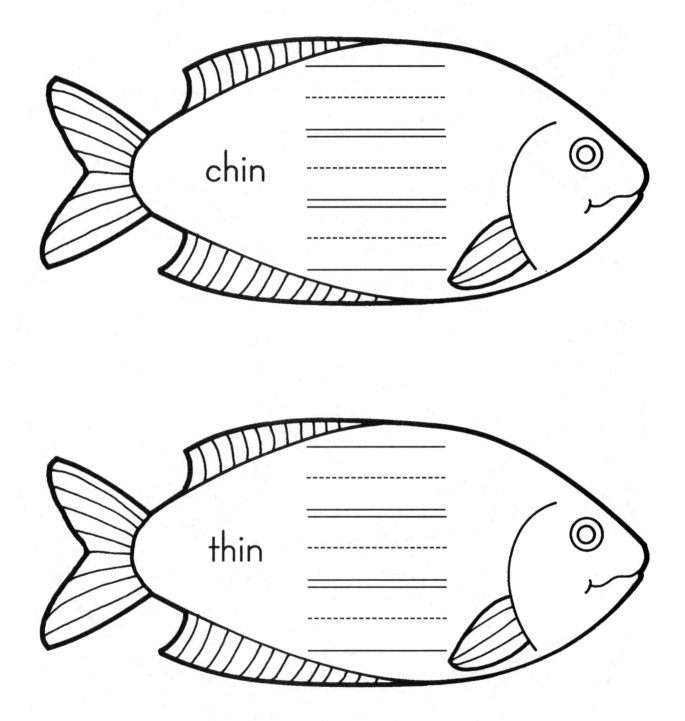

chin

thin

Write the words in ABC order in the bubbles. Color the picture.

abcdefghijklmnopqrstuvwxyz

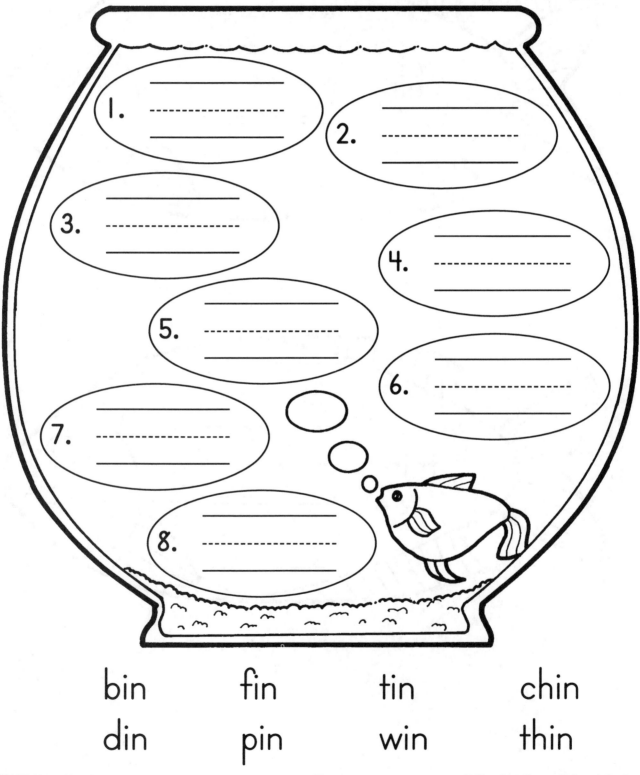

1. _____

2. _____

3. _____

4. _____

5. _____

6. _____

7. _____

8. _____

bin   fin   tin   chin

din   pin   win   thin

Color and cut out the fish. Cut out the fish's eye and the circle of letters. Put the circle behind the fish and connect them at the dot with a brad.

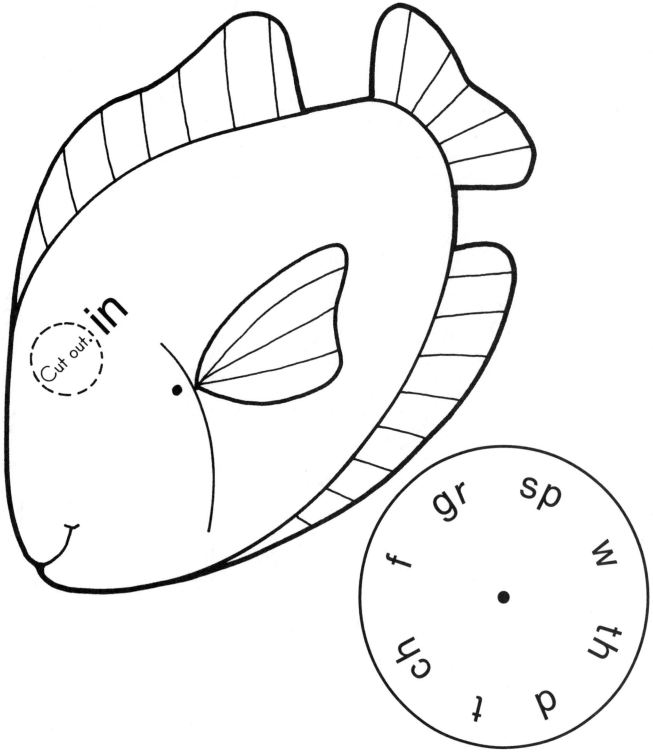

14

Circle each word in the puzzle. Color the picture.

bin

din

fin

pin

tin

thin

chin

win

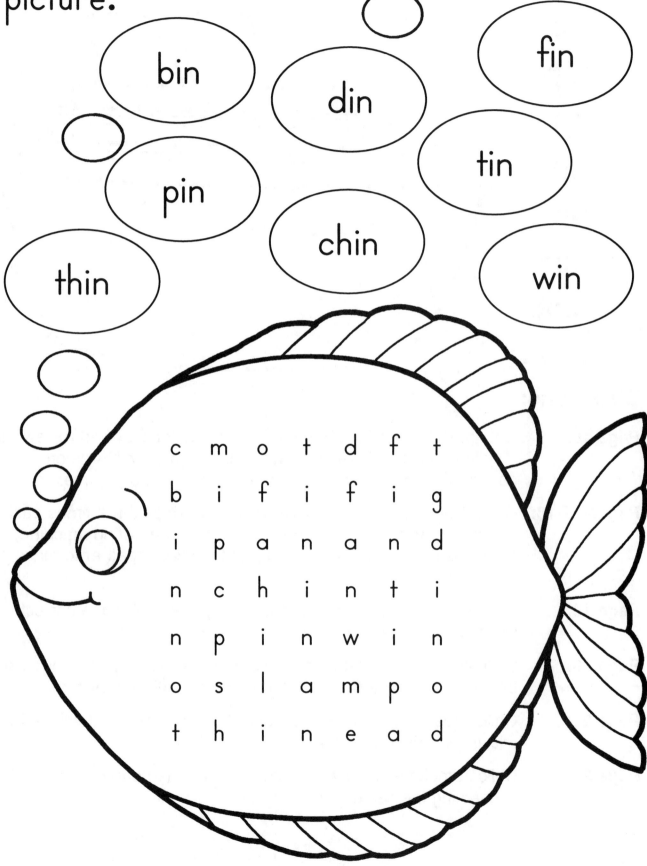

```
c  m  o  t  d  f  t
b  i  f  i  f  i  g
i  p  a  n  a  n  d
n  c  h  i  n  t  i
n  p  i  n  w  i  n
o  s  l  a  m  p  o
t  h  i  n  e  a  d
```

Common Word Family __ip

Vocabulary:

dip

hip

lip

rip

tip

flip

ship

trip

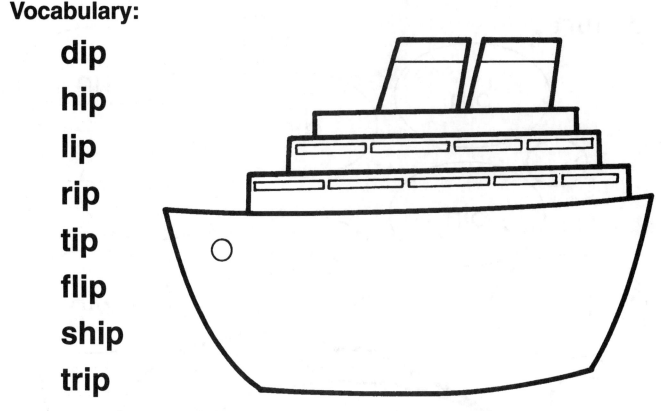

Directions:

Page 16: Cut apart the word cards on the inside back cover and review the __ip vocabulary. To extend, the child can draw pictures on corresponding cards and play a matching memory game.

Pages 17-18: Child writes the vocabulary words on the ships three times each and colors them. If you have access to a duplicating machine, the ships can be copied, cut out, and stapled together to make a book.

Page 19: Child unscrambles each word on a ship and writes the correct words on the lines provided.

Page 20: Child circles the vocabulary words in the word search. They can be found across or down. Child can then color the picture.

Page 21: Child uses the rebus clues to read the sentences and writes the missing words in the blanks.

Page 22: Child completes each word with __ip and then draws lines connecting the same words.

Write each word three times. Color the ships.

dip

_____   _____   _____

hip

_____   _____   _____

lip

_____   _____   _____

rip

_____   _____   _____

Write each word three times. Color the ships.

tip

flip

ship

trip

Unscramble the words. Write them correctly on the lines.

 ipt _____

 trpi _____

 pih _____

 pil _____

 hpis _____

 pid _____

 fpil _____

 rpi _____

| dip | ship | flip | rip |
| trip | hip | tip | lip |

Circle the words in the puzzle. Color the picture.

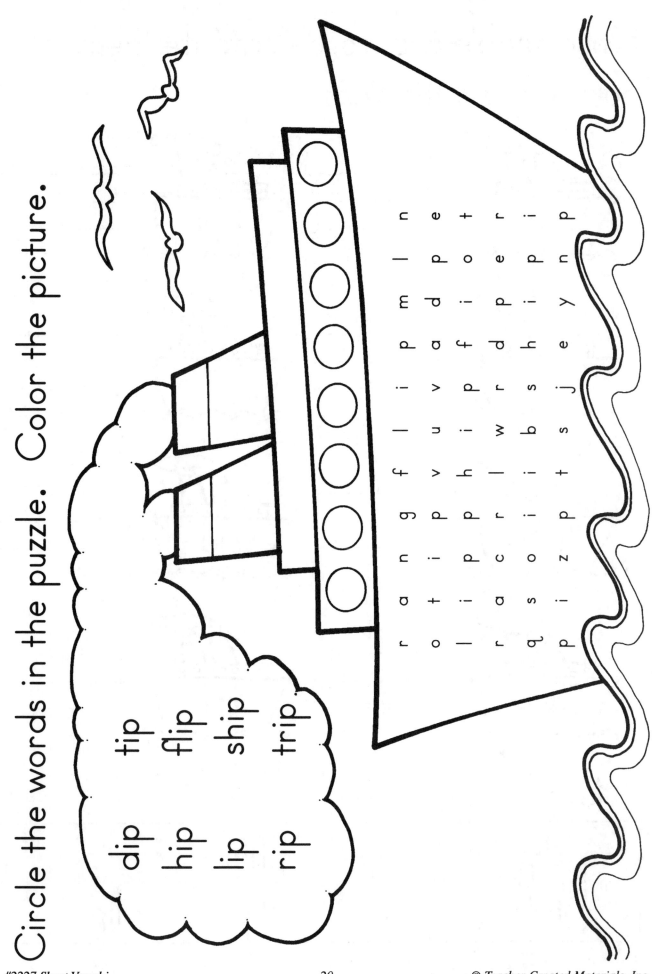

dip   tip

hip   flip

lip   ship

rip   trip

Read the sentences. Write the missing words in the blanks.

1. I will go for a _____ .

2. I can do a _____ .

3. This is a _____ .

4. We will take a _____ .

5. I will go on a _____ .

6. This is a _____ .

7. It has a _____ .

8. I will go to the _____ .

dip	lip	tip	ship
hip	rip	flip	trip

Finish each word with **ip.** Draw a line to match the same words.

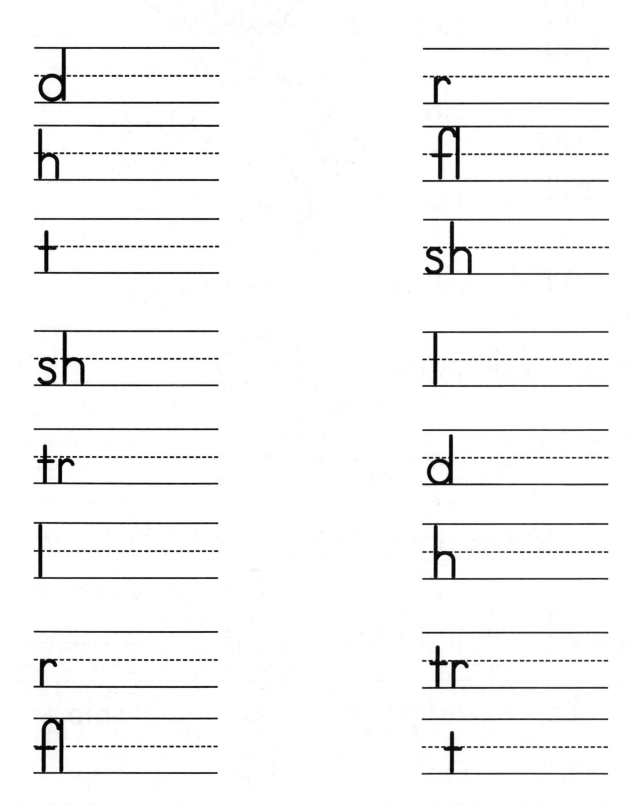

d

h

t

sh

tr

l

r

fl

r

fl

sh

l

d

h

tr

t

Common Word Family __ill

Vocabulary:

bill

fill

hill

ill

mill

pill

will

still

Directions:

Page 23: Cut apart the word cards on the inside back cover and review the __ill vocabulary. To extend, the child can draw pictures on corresponding cards and play a matching memory game.

Pages 24-26: Child writes the vocabulary words on the windmills three times each and colors them. If you have access to a duplicating machine, the windmills can be copied, cut out, and stapled together to make a book.

Page 27: Child unscrambles each word on a windmill and writes the correct words on the lines provided.

Page 28: Child writes the words on the windmills in alphabetical order. Child can then color the picture.

Page 29: Child writes __ill on the eight blanks, forming the vocabulary words. Child then makes a pinwheel that works like a windmill. Child cuts out the pattern along the dotted lines and folds down the corners so that the four dots connect with the center dot. Press a push pin through the center dot and into the top of a pencil's eraser. (The pencil then becomes the stick for the pinwheel.)

Write each word on the windmills three times. Color the windmills.

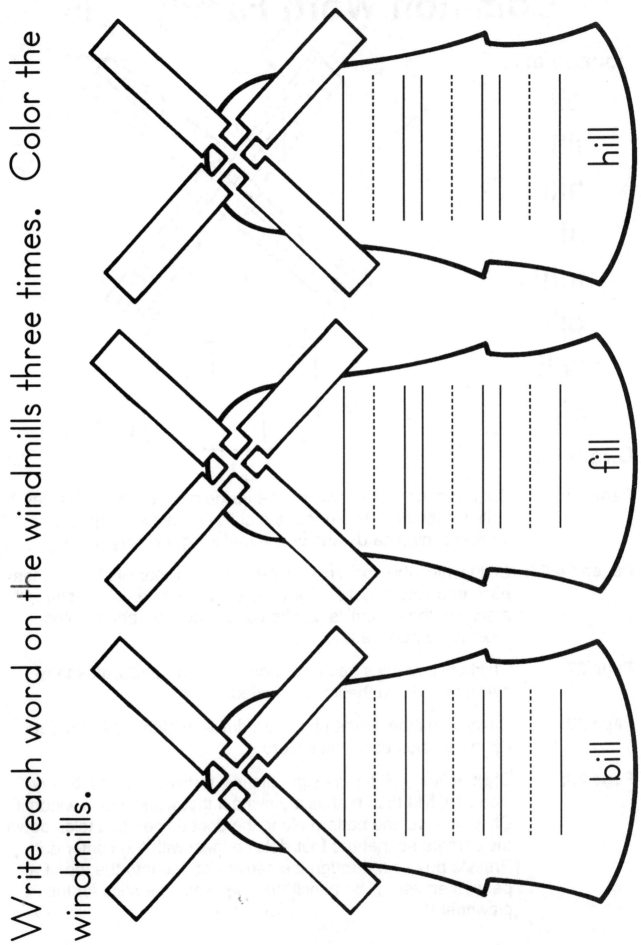

hill

fill

bill

Write each word on the windmills three times. Color the windmills.

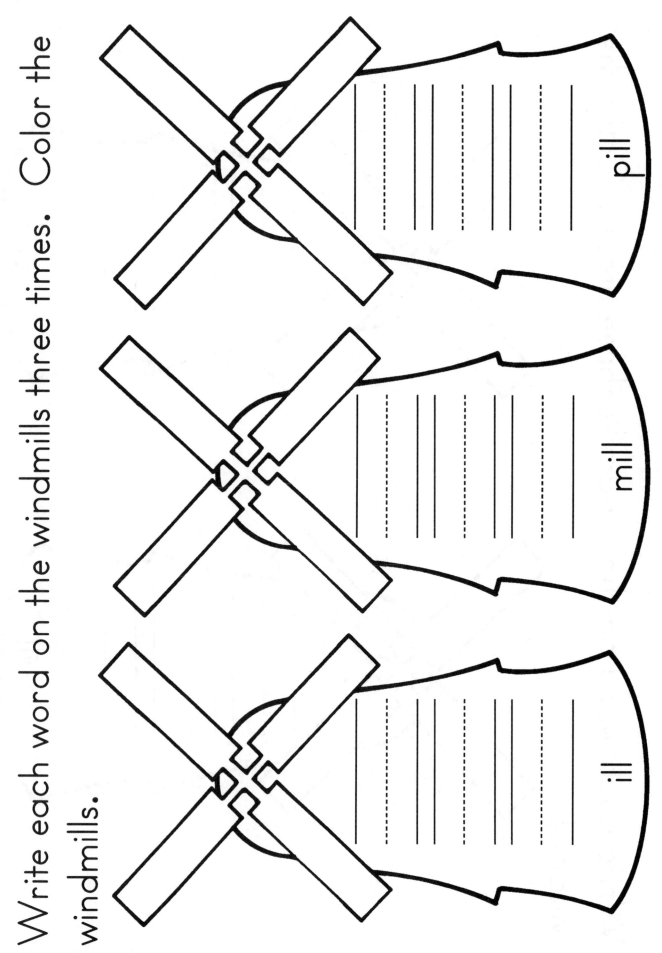

pill

mill

ill

Write each word on the windmills three times. Color the windmills.

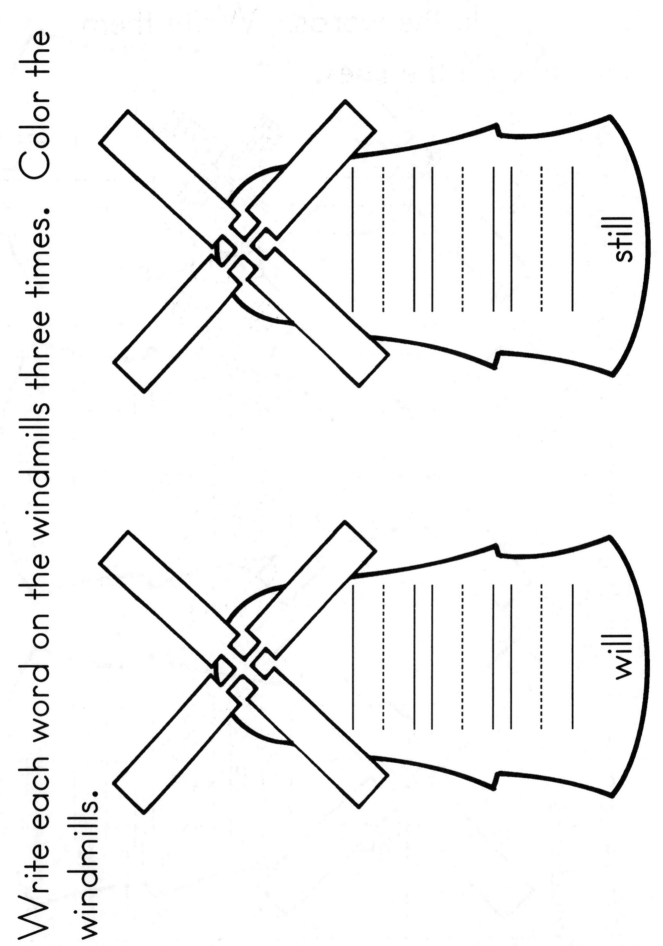

still

will

Unscramble the words. Write them correctly on the lines.

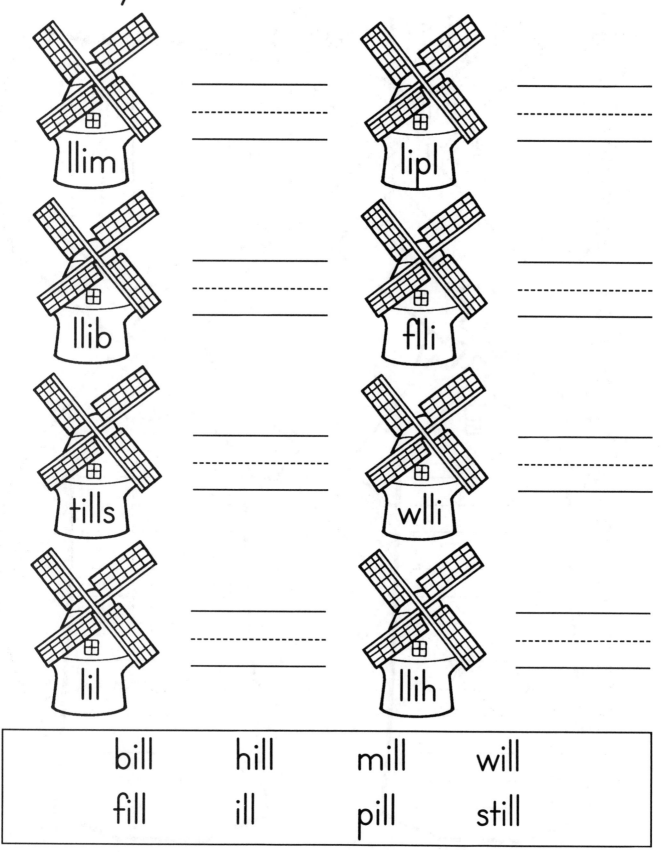

llim _____	lipl _____
llib _____	flli _____
tills _____	wlli _____
lil _____	llih _____

bill	hill	mill	will
fill	ill	pill	still

Write the words on the windmills in ABC order. Color the windmills.

abcdefghijklmnopqrstuvwxyz

will   pill   ill   still

bill   fill   mill   hill

1. _____

2. _____

3. _____

4. _____

5. _____

6. _____

7. _____

8. _____

Make a pinwheel that works like a windmill.

1. Write **ill** after each letter.
2. Cut on all the dashed lines.
3. Fold each section so that the dots meet at the center.
4. Have an adult help you press a pushpin through the center and into the top of a pencil's eraser.

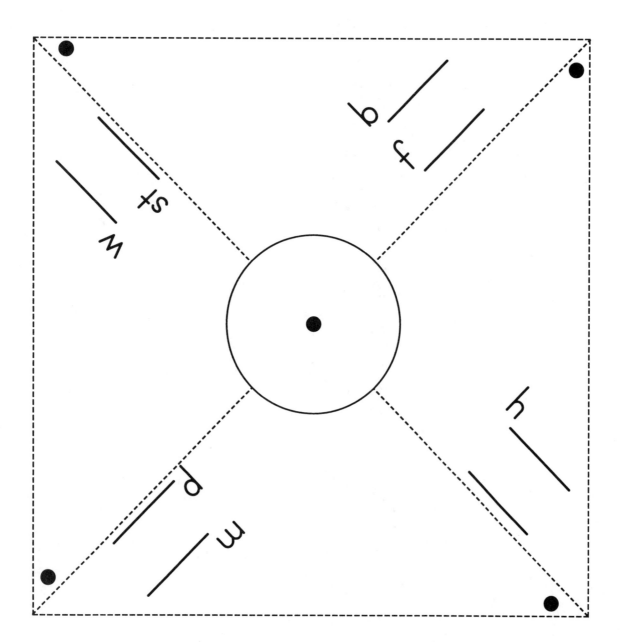

Write the words in the correct word family.

sit	win	pit	trip	chin	dip	din	bill
lip	fit	hip	fin	slit	fill	flip	kit
hit	pin	rip	ill	hill	tip	lit	bin
tin	pill	mill	bit	will	ship	thin	still

___it

___in

___ip

___ill

Finish each word with **it** or **in**.

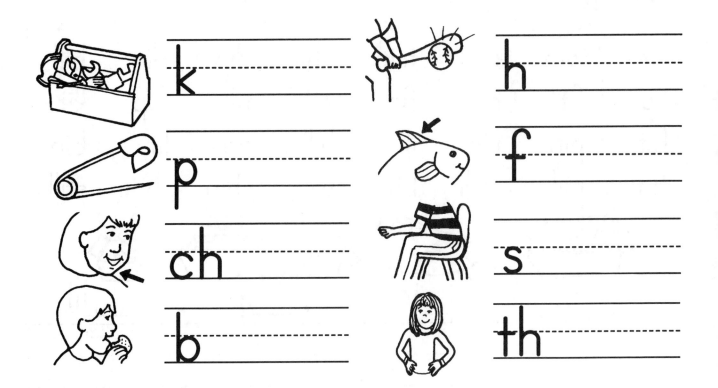

k _ _ _ _ _ _ _ _   h _ _ _ _ _ _ _ _

p _ _ _ _ _ _ _ _   f _ _ _ _ _ _ _ _

ch _ _ _ _ _ _ _   s _ _ _ _ _ _ _ _

b _ _ _ _ _ _ _ _   th _ _ _ _ _ _ _

Finish each word with **ip** or **ill**.

l _ _ _ _ _ _ _ _   p _ _ _ _ _ _ _ _

sh _ _ _ _ _ _ _   r _ _ _ _ _ _ _ _

m _ _ _ _ _ _ _ _   h _ _ _ _ _ _ _ _

b _ _ _ _ _ _ _ _   h _ _ _ _ _ _ _ _